THREAD TALK

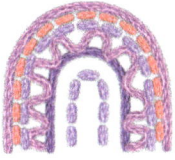

GUIDE TO IDENTIFYING
HEALTHY RELATIONSHIPS

Hannah Kay Herdlinger

SPARK Publications
Charlotte, North Carolina

I0096380

Thread Talk
Guide to Identifying Healthy Relationships

Hannah Kay Herdlinger

Copyright ©2023 by Hannah Kay Herdlinger. All rights reserved.
No part of this book may be used or reproduced in any manner
whatsoever without written permission from the author, except
in the case of brief quotations embodied in critical articles or
reviews. For permissions requests, please contact the author at
hannahkay@threadtalk.com.

Designed, produced, and published by SPARK Publications
SPARKpublications.com
Charlotte, North Carolina

Printed in the United States of America

Paperback, February 2023, ISBN: 978-1-953555-43-4
Library of Congress Control Number: 2023901001

This book is dedicated to all the

YOUNG AND WISE WOMEN

of today

WITH HOPES AND WISHES

for your

HEALTHY, SAFE & LOVING

relationships of tomorrow

TABLE OF CONTENTS

WELCOME

Hello Superstar,

Congratulations on taking the first step in identifying healthy relationships in your life! If you are anything like me, you'll try to hurry through this guide so you can check the box. Trust me, I know! I thought the exact same thing the first time someone tried to teach me about healthy relationships.

Why are healthy relationships important? I'm glad you asked! Healthy relationships are a vital component of your overall health and well-being. They can decrease stress and lead to a longer life. Relationships should be mutually life-giving—not soul-sucking and toxic. Toxic relationships cause feelings of low self-worth, helplessness, fear, anxiety, depression, and stress. Stress shortens your life span.

No relationship is perfect and there are always things that you can work on. However, you should always feel safe in a relationship, feel equal with your partner, and feel respect for each other. While this guide focuses on dating partners, these principles apply to relationships with friends, family, spouses, and coworkers.

> NO RELATIONSHIP IS PERFECT AND THERE ARE ALWAYS THINGS THAT YOU CAN WORK ON. HOWEVER, YOU SHOULD ALWAYS FEEL SAFE IN A RELATIONSHIP, FEEL EQUAL WITH YOUR PARTNER, AND FEEL RESPECT FOR EACH OTHER.

Who am I and why should you trust this guide? There are a few things I say when I meet someone new. First and foremost, I tell people my name is Hannah Kay Herdlinger. Then I tell them I go by my first and middle name together: Hannah Kay. People in the South get that. People everywhere else? Not so much. Next, I tell people I'm the founder of a company called Thread Talk, which sells the softest blankets you've ever felt. And Thread Talk donates 10 percent of each purchase to DomesticShelters.org to fund critical wish list items for domestic violence shelters across the country.

Then, I tell them I started Thread Talk because I am a domestic violence survivor. It's not something I ever thought I would say about myself—especially not written in a book for all to see. But then again, it's not a title I ever thought I would hold.

No one grows up dreaming of being the victim of any kind of violence— let alone violence that comes from someone we love, often more than anyone. But when it happened to me (and I'll get to that in a moment), I certainly wasn't going to talk about it. My close friends and family knew. They helped me leave. My boss knew. She helped me start a brand-new life three thousand miles away. But that was it. I wasn't telling anyone else. Domestic violence was my secret, and I was going to hold it as close as I possibly could.

> " I'VE LEARNED THAT WORDS ARE POWERFUL; THE WORDS WE CHOOSE TO SAY OUT LOUD ARE EVEN MORE POWERFUL. THAT'S WHY I TELL EVERYONE I AM A DOMESTIC VIOLENCE SURVIVOR—NOT A VICTIM. NEVER A VICTIM.

That's not the case now. I've learned that words are powerful; the words we choose to say out loud are even more powerful. That's why I tell everyone I am a domestic violence *survivor*—not a victim. Never a victim.

In that simple phrase of *domestic violence survivor*—one so many of us would never dare to say out loud—I have given myself permission to own not what happened to me, but to own what I've done as a result. That's the first step toward empowerment: give yourself permission to be more than you think you can be. Or as I tell women all the time: Go Break Plates.

I have to confess, it's a phrase I stole from another survivor who came to my house in the early days after I left my husband. She sat down in my kitchen and told me that part of my recovery would involve going through the five stages of grief. You may know these. First there's denial, then anger. Anger is followed by bargaining, then depression, until you finally come to acceptance.

> **" BY TELLING ME TO GO BREAK PLATES, THIS WOMAN GAVE ME PERMISSION TO BE LOUD AND MESSY, HONEST AND REAL. THAT WAS EXACTLY WHAT I NEEDED TO HEAR AT EXACTLY THE RIGHT TIME.**

Anger was the stage that stood out for the woman in my kitchen. When she hit that particular stage of grief, she walked into her kitchen, pulled all the plates out of her cupboards, and smashed them—every single one. She told me that if you get to the anger stage and you want to break some plates, do it. So many survivors come through those abusive relationships and shut down. They hide. They feel ashamed, as though what happened was their fault, when in fact it was quite the opposite.

However, by telling me to go break plates, this woman gave me permission to be loud and messy, honest and real. That was exactly what I needed to hear at exactly the right time. I had permission to be more than I thought I could. I also knew I wasn't alone. Soon enough, I would discover just how many of us are out there.

The statistics around domestic violence in this country are stunning: one in four women and one in ten men in the US have experienced sexual violence, physical violence, or stalking by an intimate partner in their lifetime. Among adult victims of rape, physical violence, and/or stalking by an intimate partner, 22 percent of women and 15 percent of men first experienced some form of partner violence between 11 and 17 years of age.

One in four women; one in ten men. I am not the only one with a story to tell.

But I'm writing this now, so I'll take the lead. My hope is that it will change your perception of what domestic violence looks like. And for my fellow survivors, I hope it will encourage you to go break plates.

I was born and raised in the South. I graduated from the University of Georgia, and then I moved to Washington, DC, to start my career in government. First I landed an internship with Senator Blanche Lincoln of Arkansas. That's where I started to learn the ins and outs of politics—and I loved it. I networked with the other staffers on Capitol Hill and set my sights on my next career goal.

I wanted to be a scheduler to Senator Mark Pryor. That may not sound like a glamorous job in politics, but think about it: you are the gatekeeper to a member of the United States Senate. No one gets in to see him or her without going through you first. You have great power, but also great responsibility. And I wanted in. So I continued networking, making the right connections that would spark the right conversations. I was working the system, as any good politician does. And I got the job. I became the youngest scheduler in the US Senate.

For six years, that was my life. I was working hard and building a career. But I was also getting a little antsy. Six years is a long time in the life of a quasi-millennial. And when the right opportunity came along, I left.

> " FOR SIX YEARS, THAT WAS MY LIFE. I WAS WORKING HARD AND BUILDING A CAREER. BUT I WAS ALSO GETTING A LITTLE ANTSY. SIX YEARS IS A LONG TIME IN THE LIFE OF A QUASI-MILLENNIAL. AND WHEN THE RIGHT OPPORTUNITY CAME ALONG, I LEFT.

That opportunity was with Facebook. It was 2011. Facebook wasn't yet a public company, but it was the dominant force in social networking. And I was a cross-functional team member working out of the DC office.

Because this is where my life changed forever, I'm going to pause for a moment to add in a detail I didn't mention earlier. Back when I was a student at the University of Georgia, I met a guy the first week of class and we fell in love. When I moved to DC, he followed; then we got married. We built this amazing and wonderful life together, and I felt like I had everything I could have ever wanted.

Not long after I started my job at Facebook, he had an opportunity back in Georgia. We decided to move back to his tiny little hometown. We bought my dream house, and Facebook agreed to let me continue my role remotely.

Perfection, right? At the time, I hoped that was what it looked like—what I made it look like—to our friends and family and neighbors.

" WE BUILT THIS AMAZING AND WONDERFUL LIFE TOGETHER, AND I FELT LIKE I HAD EVERYTHING I COULD HAVE EVER WANTED.

Perfection these days has suffered a fall from grace. I think we can thank a bunch of highly curated social media profiles for that. Perfection is being replaced by this push for authenticity. Who are we really? And can we show that side of ourselves to the world, please?

That wasn't the case back then, so I was telling the story I wanted everyone around me to hear. But that story was far from my reality. I don't know how long I could have kept up the facade, but in the end, it wasn't a choice I got to make.

It was Super Bowl Sunday. I wanted to have a chicken wing in one hand and a beer in the other while debating the finer points of million-dollar commercials. But I didn't. I was arguing with my husband. Again.

And it got violent. Again.

It could have been a normal fight—"normal" meaning the kinds of bruises and marks I'd grown accustomed to hiding or explaining away. But this was not a normal fight. It was the worst violence I've ever experienced. He hit me hard in the head, multiple times. He sat on me, pinning me down, leaving me with bruised ribs and a black-and-blue face. And I ended up in the hospital. The doctor told me if I had been hit a little harder, or if I had been struck a little to the right, I could have ended up in a coma.

I also could have died.

That moment was the lowest point of my life. I had known for some time I needed to get out of that relationship, but that's the problem with domestic violence. It always comes from someone you love, which makes it hard to do what you know you must. But this—the doctors, the confessions to friends and family, the pain—this was a wake-up call like nothing I'd ever experienced.

That doesn't mean leaving was easy. As any domestic violence survivor will tell you, leaving is only easy to those on the outside. You're in a destructive relationship; just walk away, right? But consider this: Domestic violence survivors can feel isolated, depressed, helpless, and ashamed. We're afraid of being judged or stigmatized. We are often financially dependent on our abusers. We may have religious or cultural beliefs that reinforce staying in the relationship. We may not have any support from friends or family.

> " THAT'S THE PROBLEM WITH DOMESTIC VIOLENCE. IT ALWAYS COMES FROM SOMEONE YOU LOVE, WHICH MAKES IT HARD TO DO WHAT YOU KNOW YOU MUST.

And how do you leave when you have nowhere to turn?

My decision was made easier by the fact that I received unending support from friends and family—even my boss at the time, Facebook's chief operating officer Sheryl Sandberg. I called to tell her what happened and to ask for some time to recover. Instead, she offered me a job at Facebook headquarters and a chance to restart my life three thousand miles from home.

And I took that chance. But before I left Georgia, I did one last thing that would later have an immense impact on my life: I packed up my house and donated the entire contents to a local domestic violence shelter.

For so many survivors, shelters are a lifeline. More than a just a roof and a bed, shelters provide safety, security, and programs to help survivors get back on their feet. In the years since I left my marriage, I've met hundreds of women who have passed through shelters on their way out of abusive relationships. And for every single one of them, their shelter played a critical part in helping them break free.

I thought about that shelter in Georgia when I moved to Silicon Valley and began my job at Facebook. I kept thinking about it when Sheryl asked me to serve as director of operations for her nonprofit, Lean In. And one day, when Sheryl delivered what has since become a well-known speech to the UC Berkeley graduating class, all of those thoughts came to a head.

In her speech, Sheryl challenged the graduates to live as if they had only eleven days left on the earth. She urged them to live with the understanding of how precious every single day would be. And I listened to her, tears falling down my face. In that moment I realized, while I had a great job with an admirable mission, I wasn't doing what I wanted with my life. I wanted to be back closer to home. And I wanted to help victims of domestic violence find their way to better lives.

Of course, nothing in life happens in a straight line. On my way back east, I detoured a bit. I spent some time working on Hillary Clinton's presidential campaign, and then I helped Arianna Huffington launch her new venture, Thrive Global in New York. It was good to be around powerful, successful women. And I realized something: I was one too.

" WHEN I VISITED THAT FIRST SHELTER BACK IN GEORGIA, I LEARNED THAT BLANKETS AND LINENS ARE SOME OF THE MOST IN-DEMAND ITEMS AT SHELTERS ACROSS THE COUNTRY. THERE WAS SOMETHING POETIC ABOUT THAT.

When I got to Charlotte, North Carolina, I didn't know a soul, so I started putting myself out there, building connections, and asking for help. Then I broke some plates and started my business, Thread Talk.

When I visited that first shelter back in Georgia, I learned that blankets and linens are some of the most in-demand items at shelters across the country. There was something poetic about that. Blankets are a source of warmth, certainly, but they are also a source of comfort and security. The thought of wrapping up yourself in a soft, cozy blanket just makes you feel better. Like a warm cup of tea on a cold day.

I did a little more digging and learned that, yes, blankets and linens are in high demand, but every shelter is different. Some need cleaning supplies or kitchen items or envelopes. There's a shelter in the Charlotte region right now in urgent need of saltines—seriously. The simplest gifts would mean everything to a shelter that is scrambling to provide life-saving services to its residents.

So I put together a business plan that merged the beautiful poetry of blankets with those raw, everyday needs. I would sell blankets—beautiful, soft, luxurious blankets that anyone would love—and I would donate a portion of the proceeds to DomesticShelters.org, an organization that provides critical wish list items to domestic violence shelters across the country.

> " BLANKETS ARE A SOURCE OF WARMTH, CERTAINLY, BUT THEY ARE ALSO A SOURCE OF COMFORT AND SECURITY. THE THOUGHT OF WRAPPING UP YOURSELF IN A SOFT, COZY BLANKET JUST MAKES YOU FEEL BETTER. LIKE A WARM CUP OF TEA ON A COLD DAY.

There was just one problem: I knew absolutely nothing about making blankets. I knew even less about selling them. I was a speech communications major with a weird, winding career through politics and social media. I knew nothing about business.

This brings me to the best business lesson I've learned to date: own your ignorance. I called up manufacturers in all parts of the world and told them straight up: "I know nothing about making blankets. What do I need to know?"

You might think that would open me up to a bunch of scammers and shady business dealings, but you'd be surprised how many good people there are in the world. Almost every person I spoke to was kind and helpful, and generous with their time. Something about honesty makes it so much easier to build strong connections.

In October 2017, I launched Thread Talk. I had a website, I had blankets, and I had a mission; but I needed customers. And anyone who has tried to stand out in the crowded e-commerce space knows that finding customers is no easy feat. I had no marketing budget. I had no employees. It was me, a handful of really good friends, and some amazing volunteers.

Since that launch, the Thread Talk mission has expanded. Yes, we want to help provide shelters with the everyday items they need. But we also want to empower domestic violence survivors and others (like you) to identify the green flags of healthy relationships, as well as to recognize the red flags of unhealthy relationships *before* those warning signs escalate to violence—which could lead to death.

We now have Thread Talk Trailblazers: college students who want to become pillars in their community in the fight against domestic violence. They promote Thread Talk and initiate conversations about healthy relationships on campuses across the country.

We're giving people permission to go break plates. And it's amazing what happens when they do.

" WE WANT TO HELP PROVIDE SHELTERS WITH THE EVERYDAY ITEMS THEY NEED. BUT WE ALSO WANT TO EMPOWER DOMESTIC VIOLENCE SURVIVORS AND OTHERS (LIKE YOU) TO IDENTIFY THE GREEN FLAGS OF HEALTHY RELATIONSHIPS.

I'm honored to know many survivors. They inspire me to continue the work of ending domestic violence before it even starts—and to help others get out of their current abusive relationships.

The following pages have been carefully curated for you to identify characteristics of your own relationships. I hope you find yourself in healthy relationships and that these signs will keep you in healthy relationships.

If you find yourself in a toxic relationship, or you notice a friend, family member, or coworker in a toxic relationship, we also have resources to support you.

Your future is so bright. Always remember: You are strong. You are loved. You are not alone.

All my love and gratitude,

Hannah Kay

YOUR FUTURE IS

BRIGHT

CHAPTER ONE

DISCOVERING YOUR CORE VALUES

"The key to genuine happiness is in our hands. To think this way is to discover the essential values of kindness, brotherly love, and altruism. The more clearly we see the benefits of these values, the more we will seek to reject anything that opposes them; in this way, we will be able to bring about inner transformation."

—His Holiness the 14th Dalai Lama[1]

Living a purposeful and fulfilling life happens when we live according to our core values and follow our own personal beliefs. Values are a part of us. They highlight what we stand for. They guide our behavior, providing us with a personal code of conduct. Values are important because they can help us grow and develop. They help us predict each other's choices and help us avoid misunderstandings, frustration, and distrust.

Not every relationship is going to have the same values. Some people might view certain values as less important than others. Everyone is different, but it is important to define what your core values are, as they can help you focus on the things that matter most to you in life. Then, when someone or something challenges your values, you will be less likely to doubt or second-guess yourself.

As you define your core values, be honest with yourself. As you read each of the following values, spend some time in personal reflection to discover what matters most to you.

---

1   His Holiness the Dalai Lama, *Beyond Dogma: Dialogues & Discourses*, trans. Alison Anderson, ed. Marianne Dresser (Berkeley, CA: North Atlantic Books, 1996), 72.

VALUES EXERCISE

Read through each word listed below and reflect on what it means to you.
Circle all of the words that best describe you.

INTEGRITY	PASSION	INDEPENDENCE
COMMITMENT	SPIRITUALITY	INDIVIDUALITY
DEPENDABILITY	CHARITY	COURAGE
HONESTY	COMMUNICATION	CLEANLINESS
RESPONSIBILITY	COMMUNITY	FAMILY
COMPASSION	EQUALITY	FRIENDSHIP
EMPATHY	PROFESSIONALISM	GENEROSITY
EMPOWERMENT	SKILLFULNESS	LOYALTY
GROWTH	SUCCESS	MATURITY
INTELLIGENCE	WEALTH	SELFLESSNESS
INSIGHT	CREATIVITY	SENSITIVITY
THOUGHTFULNESS	OPENNESS	SUPPORT
UNDERSTANDING	ORIGINALITY	SPONTANEITY
GRATITUDE	AMBITION	DECISIVENESS
HAPPINESS	CONFIDENCE	JUSTICE
KINDNESS	DEDICATION	ORGANIZATION
OPTIMISM	DISCIPLINE	

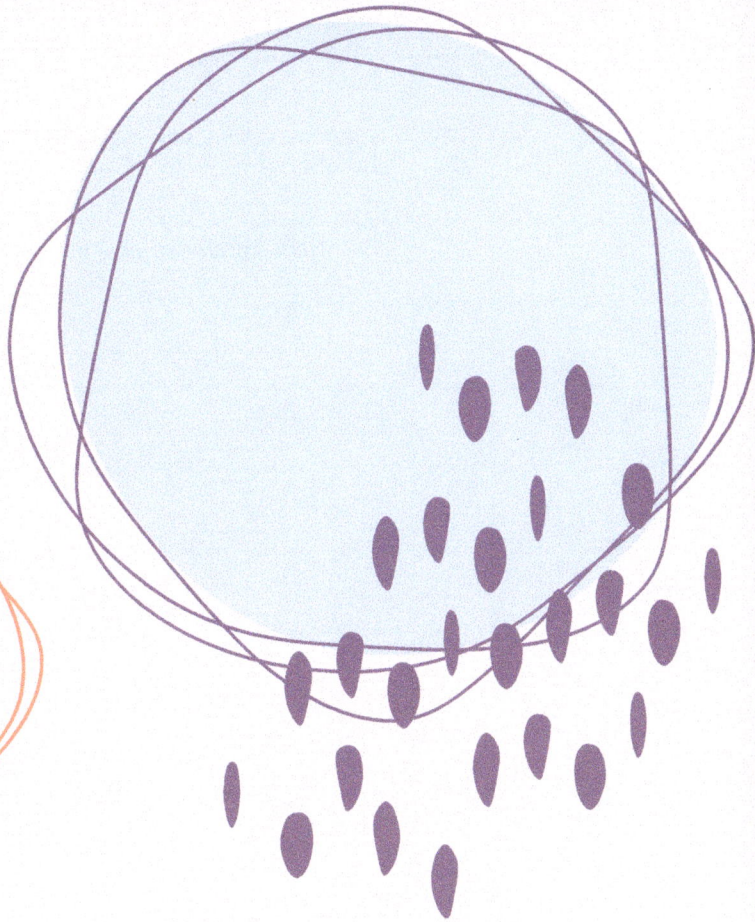

LIST YOUR TOP TEN VALUES

Now, condense your list to just your top 10.

1

2

3

4

5

6

7

8

9

10

NARROW YOUR LIST TO FIVE VALUES

Whew! That was tough, but let's whittle it down one more time. Look at your top 10 values and rank them in order of top priority. Your top 5 priority goals are your core values.

1

2

3

4

5

CHAPTER TWO

IS YOUR RELATIONSHIP HEALTHY?

GREEN FLAGS OF RELATIONSHIPS

Many people talk about relationship red flags, or warning signs that there may be problems with a relationship. But an absence of obvious red flags doesn't automatically make someone a potentially great partner. We believe that the presence of green flags—signs of a healthy relationship—is actually more important.

By focusing on green flags, you may discover how much of a positive impact your relationship has on your life, and you will be more likely to find ways to continue to grow as a couple.

TEN GREEN FLAGS
OF A RELATIONSHIP

YOU COMMUNICATE
OPENLY & EFFORTLESSLY

YOU TRUST EACH OTHER

YOU SUPPORT EACH OTHER'S
GOALS & DREAMS

YOU MAKE DECISIONS
T O G E T H E R

YOU ARGUE
WITHOUT CONSEQUENCES

YOU LOOK FORWARD TO
BEING ALONE TOGETHER

YOU FEEL EMPOWERED AND INSPIRED

YOU DON'T WORRY ABOUT
WHERE THEY ARE
OR WHO THEY ARE TALKING TO

YOU FIND YOURSELF
LAUGHING AND SMILING A LOT

YOU'RE PROUD
TO CALL THEM YOUR PARTNER

HEALTHY RELATIONSHIPS QUIZ

Everyone deserves to be in a safe and healthy relationship.
Do you know if your relationship is healthy? Take the quiz below to find out.
Partner can refer to a dating partner, spouse, friend, family member, or coworker.

Your partner is supportive.

● Yes ■ No ◗ Sometimes

Your partner encourages you to explore new activities.

● Yes ■ No ◗ Sometimes

Your partner is a good listener.

● Yes ■ No ◗ Sometimes

Your friends like to be around your partner.

● Yes ■ No ◗ Sometimes

Your partner encourages you to focus on your self-care

(e.g., appearance, time alone, healthy habits).

● Yes ■ No ◗ Sometimes

Your partner is never envious or resentful.

● Yes ■ No ◗ Sometimes

Your partner trusts you.

● Yes ■ No ◗ Sometimes

You and your partner communicate openly and respectfully.

● Yes ■ No ◢ Sometimes

Your partner encourages you to communicate with friends and family.

● Yes ■ No ◢ Sometimes

Your partner never belittles you or makes you feel less than enough.

● Yes ■ No ◢ Sometimes

Your partner has never threatened to harm you or the ones you love.

● Yes ■ No ◢ Sometimes

Your partner has never threatened to kill themselves if you break up with them.

● Yes ■ No ◢ Sometimes

Your partner respects you and your belongings.

● Yes ■ No ◢ Sometimes

Your partner makes you feel safe and secure.

● Yes ■ No ◢ Sometimes

Your partner has never physically harmed you
(pushed, slapped, punched, etc).

● Yes   ■ No   ◖ Sometimes

Your partner has never physically tried to intimidate you by throwing or destroying things.

● Yes   ■ No   ◖ Sometimes

Your partner always has your consent before sexual activities.

● Yes   ■ No   ◖ Sometimes

Your partner respects your privacy
(e.g., doesn't check your computer or phone without your knowledge).

● Yes   ■ No   ◖ Sometimes

You partner understands if you are unable to text back immediately.

● Yes   ■ No   ◖ Sometimes

Your partner doesn't control who you follow or like on social media.

● Yes   ■ No   ◖ Sometimes

RESULTS

If you answered "yes" to all of these questions: Congratulations! You are experiencing green flags—positive signs of a healthy relationship. A healthy relationship takes effort and compromise from both people. It brings out the best in you and makes you feel good about yourself. A healthy relationship does not mean a "perfect" relationship, but healthy relationships share some characteristics: mutual respect, honest communication, trust, boundaries, and consent. You should strive for all of your relationships to be healthy! Continue reading this guide to understand the different types of abuse, available resources, and ways to support a friend or roommate dealing with an abusive relationship.

If you answered "sometimes" or "no" to any of these questions: You are experiencing signs of an unhealthy relationship. If you stay, be aware that an unhealthy relationship can quickly escalate into an abusive relationship. You should always feel safe and equal with your partner. Unhealthy relationships often include some of these characteristics: lack of trust, disrespect, possessiveness, and little communication. Continue reading this guide to learn more about the different types of abuse to look out for in your relationship.

If you answered "no" to the majority of these questions: You are definitely experiencing red flags—signs of an abusive relationship. Did you know that not all abusive relationships are physically violent? In fact, emotional abuse is even more common than physical abuse. Abusive relationships often include some of these characteristics: intimidation, isolation, manipulation, use of force, no common ground, lack of mutual respect, and poor communication. Your safety is of the utmost importance! Continue reading this guide to find information and resources that can help; this guide will also help you reach out to a trusted friend and create a safety plan (Safety Planning, pagespage 88 - page 89). Always remember that you are strong, you are loved, and you are not alone.

CHAPTER THREE

POWER AND CONTROL WHEEL

The Power and Control Wheel is a tool that helps explain the different ways an abusive partner can use power and control to manipulate you in your relationship. The wheel was created by the Domestic Abuse Intervention Programs as part of "The Duluth Model," which focuses on training and education to teach communities to work together, with the goal of holding abusers accountable while improving support for survivors.

Abuse always involves control. It is never something that is deserved.

This diagram helps survivors tangibly recognize tactics inflicted upon them, identifying the patterns of abuse and danger, and then it helps them express and articulate their experiences so that they may heal and move forward in their lives.

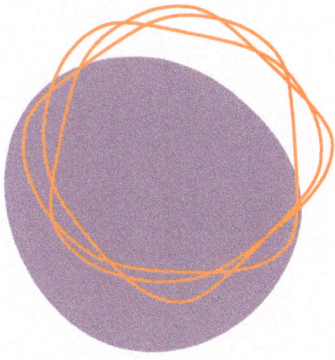
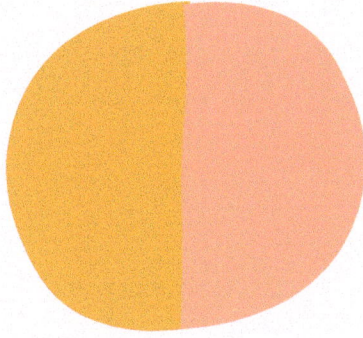

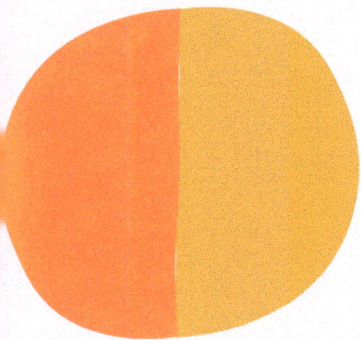

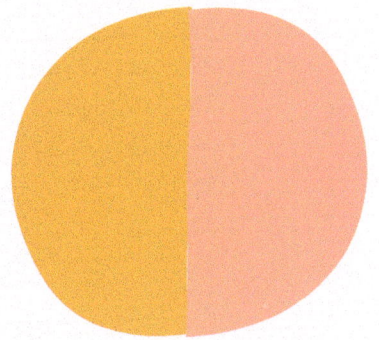

THE POWER AND CONTROL WHEEL

COERCION & THREATS

Making and/or carrying out threats to do something to hurt her. Threatening to leave her, commit suicide, or report her to welfare. Making her drop charges. Making her do illegal things.

MALE PRIVILEGE

Treating her like a servant: making all the big decisions, acting like the "master of the castle," being the one to define men's and women's roles.

ECONOMIC ABUSE

Preventing her from getting or keeping a job. Making her ask for money. Giving her an allowance. Taking her money. Not letting her know about or have access to family income.

USING CHILDREN

Making her feel guilty about the children. Using the children to relay messages. Using visitation to harass her. Threatening to take the children away.

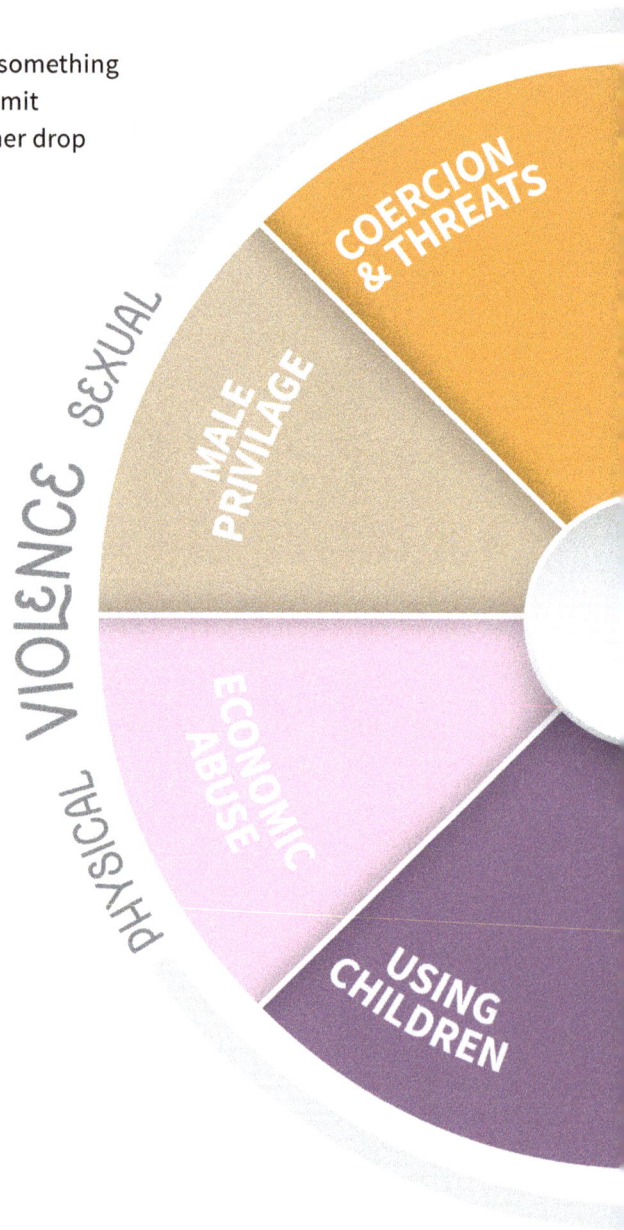

SEXUAL

PHYSICAL VIOLENCE

COERCION & THREATS

MALE PRIVILEGE

ECONOMIC ABUSE

USING CHILDREN

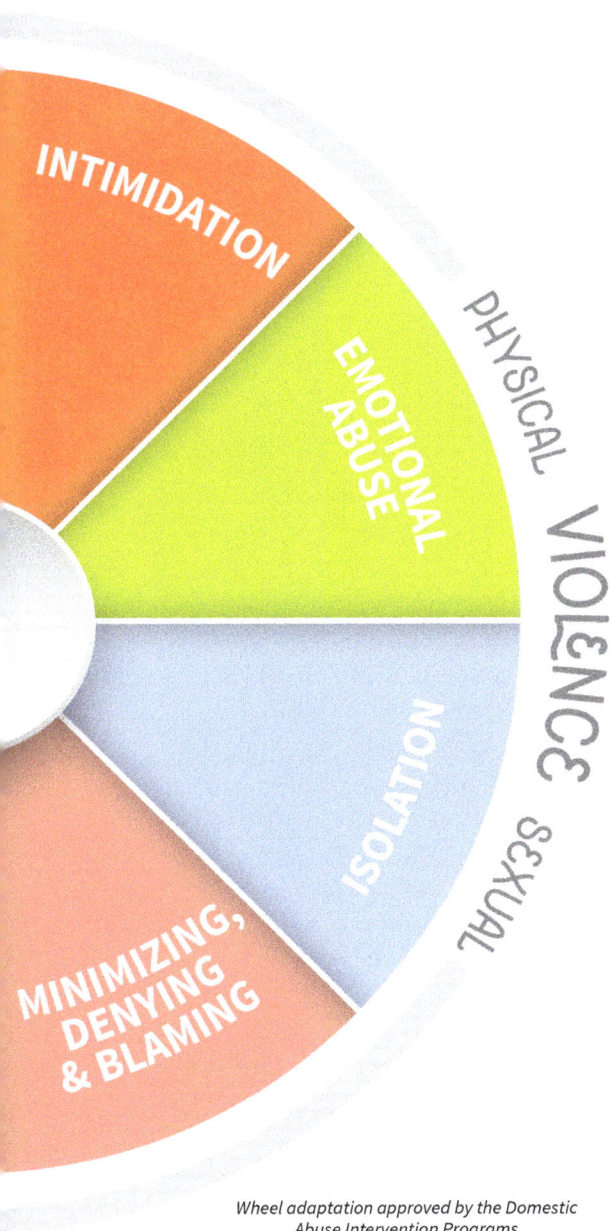

INTIMIDATION

Making her afraid by using looks, actions, and gestures. Smashing things. Destroying her property. Abusing pets. Displaying weapons.

EMOTIONAL ABUSE

Putting her down. Making her feel bad about herself. Calling her names. Making her think she's crazy. Playing mind games. Humiliating her. Making her feel guilty.

ISOLATION

Controlling what she does, who she sees and talks to, what she reads, and where she goes. Limiting her outside involvement. Using jealousy to justify actions.

MINIMIZING, DENYING & BLAMING

Making light of the abuse and not taking her concerns about it seriously. Saying the abuse didn't happen. Shifting responsibility for abusive behavior. Saying she caused it.

Wheel adaptation approved by the Domestic Abuse Intervention Programs
https://www.theduluthmodel.org/

DOMESTIC VIOLENCE STATISTICS

1 IN 4 WOMEN

1 IN 10 MEN

Experience sexual violence, physical violence, or stalking by an intimate partner during their lifetime

19,000

Number of calls domestic violence hotlines nationwide receive on a typical day

3X

Female victims sustain injuries more often than male victims

WOMEN AGED 18 - 24

Intimate partner violence is most common

$5.8 - $12.6 BILLION

Amount intimate partner violence is estimated to cost the US economy annually

These statistics are shared by the National Coalition Against Domestic Violence (2020). *Domestic violence*

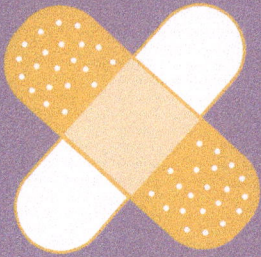

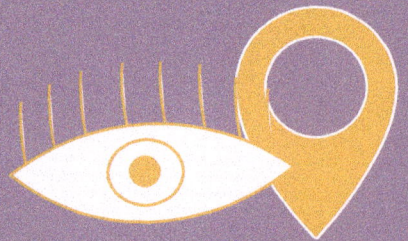

TYPES OF DATING ABUSE

Types of dating abuse descriptions and examples are courtesy of loveisrespect.org

KNOW
THAT YOU ARE
NOT ALONE

PHYSICAL

WHAT IS PHYSICAL ABUSE?

Physical abuse is any intentional, unwanted contact with you or something close to your body. It can also be any behavior that causes or intends to cause you injury, disability, or death.

Abusive behavior may not always cause physical pain or leave a bruise, but it's still unhealthy and should always be taken seriously.

EXAMPLES OF PHYSICAL ABUSE INCLUDE

- Scratching, punching, biting, strangling, choking, or kicking you
- Throwing items at you, such as a phone, book, shoe, or plate
- Pulling your hair
- Pushing or pulling you, or forcibly grabbing your clothing
- Threatening to use or actually using a gun, knife, box cutter, bat, mace, or other weapon against you
- Touching any part of you without your permission or consent
- Forcing you to have sex or perform a sexual act
- Grabbing your face to make you look at them
- Preventing you from leaving or forcing you to go somewhere

SURVIVOR STORY:
ALEXIS HUGHES

Alexis Hughes grew up in an extremely violent home. When she was three years old, her parents divorced following a series of traumatic events that included her home being set on fire by her own father. Domestic violence, assault, rape, and other horrific events became a part of Alexis's life at such a young age, and she struggled to know a life apart from that type of behavior.

Alexis's first romantic relationship was with a man who began to repeat the same behaviors she had grown accustomed to in her early years. After years of physical, mental, and financial abuse, she learned about healthy relationships, created a safety plan, and put it all into action to leave her toxic relationship.

Alexis has found a new sense of confidence in herself that has allowed her to succeed as a real estate agent—the top 1.5 percent nationwide with eXp Realty— and to empower those around her to build the type of lives they have always dreamed of. Today Alexis is happily married, raising three children with her husband and living her life to her fullest potential!

Alexis is a Thread Talk Trailblazer. Her story is told with permission.

IMPORTANT INFORMATION

Know that you are not alone. The most important thing to remember is that your partner's abusive behavior is wrong—you are deserving of a healthy, loving, and respectful relationship. Commit yourself to not making excuses for your partner's abusive behavior. Here are some steps to consider next:

1. Talk to a trusted friend, family member, or mentor.
2. Create a safety plan.
3. Obtain a restraining order.

Remember: unhealthy or abusive relationships usually get worse. It's important to assess your abusive partner's level and use of force in order to determine the urgency of your situation and what kind of support you need to be safe.

EMOTIONAL ABUSE IS
NEVER
— EVER —
YOUR FAULT

EMOTIONAL AND VERBAL

WHAT IS EMOTIONAL AND VERBAL ABUSE?

Emotional and verbal abuse includes non-physical behaviors such as threats, insults, constant monitoring or "checking in," excessive texting, humiliation, intimidation, isolation, or stalking.

EXAMPLES OF EMOTIONAL AND VERBAL ABUSE INCLUDE

- Calling you names or putting you down
- Telling you what to do or wear
- Yelling or screaming at you
- Intentionally embarrassing you in front of others or starting rumors about you
- Preventing you from seeing or communicating with friends or family, or threatening to have your children taken away from you
- Damaging your property (throwing objects, punching walls, kicking doors, etc.)
- Using online communities or communications to control, intimidate, or humiliate you
- Blaming abusive or unhealthy behavior on you or your actions
- Being jealous of outside relationships or accusing you of cheating
- Stalking you or your loved ones
- Threatening to harm you, your pet(s), or people in your life
- Gaslighting you by pretending not to understand or refusing to listen to you; questioning your recollection of facts, events, or sources; trivializing your needs or feelings; or denying previous statements or promises
- Making you feel guilty or immature when you don't consent to sexual activity
- Threatening to expose personal details, such as your sexual orientation or immigration status

shutterstock.com /oneinchpunch

SURVIVOR STORY: ALYSSA*

Alyssa was sixteen when she met Evan, the stereotypical handsome high school football player. "It was notes and sweet voicemails. He was great in the romance department. It felt like everything was too good to be true."*

Now, at thirty-five, she looks back on their young relationship and both the negative and positive effects surviving it had on her future. With fresh eyes she tries to recall the first red flag.

"I think it's when I first saw how he treated his mother. He was very rude to her, and I thought that was really odd. One day, she made him meatloaf and he yelled at her. 'You know I don't f***ing like meatloaf!' He didn't treat his dad like that." Alyssa talked herself out of her worry. "He never spoke that way to me, so I thought it must just be something complicated with his mom."

But there were other signs that raised an eyebrow for her, like Evan's entitlement. "When he turned sixteen, he expected, and got, a car. He told me, 'Your parents should be buying you a car.'"

After graduation, the two went to colleges in different cities and Evan's once-charming attribute of constant attentiveness to Alyssa took a more possessive turn. "He started calling me nonstop, wondering what I was doing and who I was with. I made the excuse that it was just because we were in a long-distance relationship."

Yet, every time they were together, Evan seemed more aggressive in his jealousy. When Alyssa would go out with her girlfriends, he would try to dictate what she wore, telling her she was dressed like a slut. When Evan hung out with Alyssa's friends, he didn't speak. He was standoffish, distant. When she'd hug a friend goodbye, he'd get angry. She thought it was odd he didn't have any close friends of his own.

"One of the big signs I remember was when we would be together and my mom would call. He told me, 'If we get married, I'd like it if you only talked to your mom once a week.'" He also seemed surprised she still talked to her friends from high school. "He'd say, 'You don't think you'll always talk to them, do you?' I kept thinking, why does he care?" At nineteen, it didn't occur to Alyssa that isolation was one of the main tactics abusers use to separate victims from their support systems. Another one is belittling, something Evan started to implement next.

"He would put me down any chance he could, saying things like I was really putting on weight and that he wasn't attracted to me as much as he used to be. He never complimented me anymore. The guy who was so romantic and sweet in the beginning was gone." She began to think that maybe she was ugly and worthless, a thought that she didn't disclose to anyone. Her self-esteem plummeted.

Alyssa's intuition told her things were getting worse. She felt like his jealousy and possessiveness were about to boil over into something more physical. Her instincts were right. One afternoon, she attended a friend's baby shower. After a few hours, she checked her cell phone and found more than forty missed calls, all from him. She called him back, worried something bad had happened. When he answered, he was furious. "Where the f*** are you?" he yelled. He didn't believe her when she told him. "I think you're f***ing lying. You're with someone," she remembers him saying.

"I hung up the phone and I knew I had to end this." She went to his house later that evening and asked him to come out on his driveway to talk to her. "I told him, 'You're not a kind man anymore and I don't want to be in this relationship.' Then, his arm went up to slap me across the face." Alyssa was able to dodge the hit with her shoulder. She was too shocked to respond, but she remembers his final words to her: "No one's going to love someone like you."

"That was it," she says, and she drove away.

Alyssa's mom would tell her later that her biggest fear was that the two of them would get married. Even though she didn't know what was going on, she had an inkling. Alyssa's lack of disclosure hurts her as a mom of a daughter herself now. "It would break my heart to not be able to help my daughter through something like that."

Does she feel like she narrowly escaped a violent future with Evan? "Absolutely. It would have only escalated and definitely would have gone physical. I think about his wife now and I fear for her and their child."

Today, married and a mom of two, Alyssa says the experience has made her stronger. "Anyone who tried to put me down or control me after that, I wouldn't allow it. I did have my guard up for a long time. I was very picky about my next relationship."

She says she and her now-husband were friends first "for a very long time," something she plans to advise her kids to do when they're ready to date. "I want them to know it's so important to be friends first, really get to know somebody, and not allow negative people into your life."

But part of her knows, no matter how much you educate someone about abuse, it can still find anyone. "You hear stories like this and think, 'I would never let that happen to me.' That's bull. You don't realize it's happening until you're in it, because it happens so slowly."

Alyssa's story originally appeared on DomesticShelters.org. It has been edited for length and reprinted with permission.

*Names changed per the interviewee's request

" TODAY, MARRIED AND A MOM OF TWO, ALYSSA SAYS THE EXPERIENCE HAS MADE HER STRONGER. "ANYONE WHO TRIED TO PUT ME DOWN OR CONTROL ME AFTER THAT, I WOULDN'T ALLOW IT. I DID HAVE MY GUARD UP FOR A LONG TIME. I WAS VERY PICKY ABOUT MY NEXT RELATIONSHIP."

IMPORTANT INFORMATION

Emotional abuse may not always cause visible harm, but it does cause emotional pain and scarring, and it may lead to physical violence eventually. Constantly being criticized, told you aren't good enough, or made to question your grasp on reality can cause you to lose confidence in yourself and lower your self-esteem. As a result, you may start to blame yourself for your partner's abusive behavior—resist this impulse.

Remember: emotional abuse is never, ever your fault. Talk to someone you trust, such as a close friend, family member, or mentor, and make a plan for your safety.

I AM HERE TODAY

— NOT —

AS A VICTIM, BUT AS A

SURVIVOR

SEXUAL

WHAT IS SEXUAL ABUSE?

Sexual abuse is any behavior that pressures or coerces someone to do something sexually that they don't want to do. It can also refer to behavior that impacts a person's ability to control their sexual activity or the circumstances in which sexual activity takes place, including oral sex, rape, or controlling reproductive methods and choices.

Everyone has the right to decide what they do or don't want to do sexually. Not all sexual assault victims know their assailant, and people of all genders and sexualities can be victims or perpetrators of sexual abuse. That includes people who are married, dating, in a "friends with benefits" arrangement, or just acquaintances.

Sexual abuse is never the victim's fault. Just because someone "didn't say no" or doesn't resist unwanted sexual advances doesn't mean that they consent. Physical resistance can sometimes put victims at higher risk for further abuse, and the narrative that a lack of resistance equals consent makes it more difficult for survivors to report abuse. It's up to each of us to understand consent and to communicate and respect the boundaries of our intimate partners, without exception.

EXAMPLES OF SEXUAL ABUSE INCLUDE

- Unwanted kissing or touching
- Unwanted rough or violent sexual activity
- Refusing to use condoms or restricting someone's access to birth control
- Preventing someone from using protection against sexually transmitted infections (STIs)
- Sexual contact with someone intoxicated from drugs or alcohol, unconscious, asleep, or otherwise unable to give clear and informed consent
- Threatening, pressuring, or otherwise forcing someone to have sex or perform sexual acts
- Using sexual insults toward someone

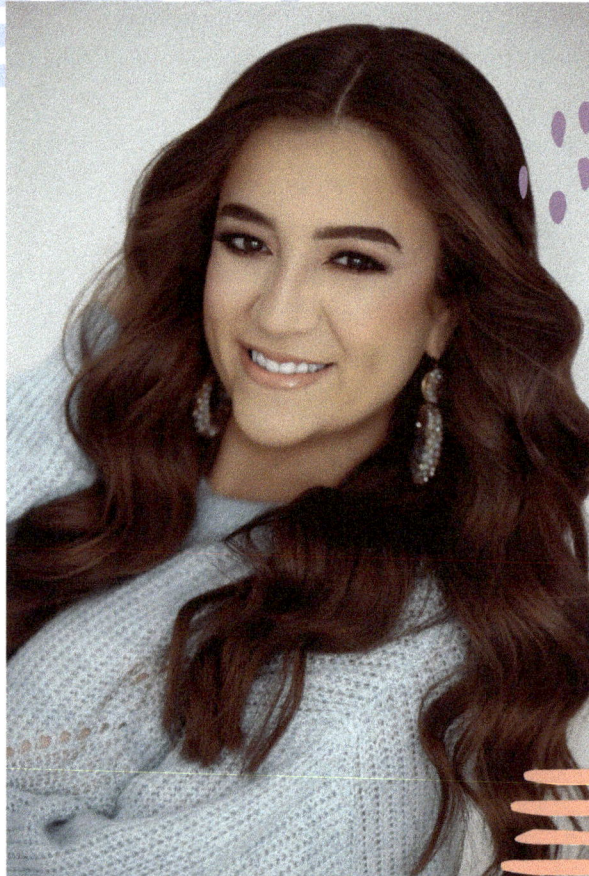

SURVIVOR STORY:
LUISA DELGADO

(I take a deep breath.)

I have won.

One in five. Every seventy-three seconds. That is how many women and how often the women experience what I did.

I have no proof. I don't even know his name. But . . . I will never forget his face or what happened. I've never spoken publicly about it before now because of fear and shame, but one year ago I was sexually assaulted. For months, I believed that if I pretended it never happened . . . then it didn't really. Right? This led to more shame and hurt, but I know that I am more than a statistic.

In the moment, I was frozen in fear but mustered up the courage to fight back. The damage had been done, but I am not damaged—and neither are the other women who aren't ready to speak up just yet.

After telling my mom for the first time about what happened, that's when my actual journey to healing began. For so long, I was carrying around this big secret that no one had known, and my parents could see that I had anxiety, which I hadn't had before. To cope was to talk about it. I think a lot of girls and people go through something like this—whether it is domestic violence, sexual assault, or rape—but society doesn't make it OK for us to talk about it, which is a big problem. But when you finally open up the conversation, you really learn that you aren't alone, that there's always someone willing to listen.

We strengthen people who have experienced sexual assault and improve today's world by putting an end to victim blaming and by reminding people that no means no.

*I am here today **not** as a victim, but as a **survivor** sharing my story with all of you. Because if I can change one, inspire one, or help just one person, then I have won.*

Luisa is a Thread Talk Trailblazer. Her story is told with permission.

IMPORTANT INFORMATION

Your safety should always be your first priority. Try to get to a safe place away from your attacker where you can think through your next steps. You may be scared, angry, confused, and hurt—remember that the abuse was not your fault.

Contact someone you trust. You may be in shock after having been sexually assaulted, and you will almost certainly feel a mix of complex emotions. Having someone there to support you can help you express and process these feelings in a way that doesn't threaten your safety, and can give you room to focus on your healing while they help with everything else. It's often useful to speak with a counselor, sexual assault hotline, or support group if you don't feel comfortable reaching out to a friend or family member.

Go to an emergency room or health clinic. It's extremely important for you to seek health care as soon as you can after being assaulted. You can expect to be treated for any injuries, offered medications to help prevent pregnancy and STIs, and have tests run to ensure your long-term well-being. There may also be sexual assault advocates in the area who can assist you and answer any questions. A Sexual Assault Nurse Examiner (SANE) can provide these services and collect evidence in case you decide to pursue legal action in the future.

Report what happened. If you determine that it's safe for you to do so, you may report what happened to law enforcement to pursue criminal legal recourse against your attacker. If you decide to do so, it's important that you do your best to avoid altering or destroying any evidence of the attack to prepare a stronger legal case. That means don't shower, wash your hair or body, comb your hair, or change your clothes, even if it's hard not to. If you're nervous about going to the police station, it may help to bring a trusted friend with you, keeping in mind any relevant safety considerations for them as well.

NO ONE

SHOULD CONTROL YOUR

ABILITY

TO WORK

FINANCIAL

WHAT IS FINANCIAL ABUSE?

Financial abuse often operates in more subtle ways than other forms of abuse, but it can be just as harmful to those who experience it. Modern conditions of stark economic inequality mean that financial security is directly tied to our health and well-being. No one has the right to use money or decide how you choose to spend it in order to control your actions or decisions, and no one should control your ability to work.

EXAMPLES OF FINANCIAL ABUSE INCLUDE

- Giving you an allowance or monitoring what you buy
- Depositing your paycheck into an account you can't access
- Preventing you from seeing shared bank accounts or records
- Forbidding you from working or limiting the hours you do
- Preventing you from going to work by taking your car, keys, or other mode of transportation
- Getting you fired by harassing you, your employer, or your coworkers
- Hiding or stealing your student financial aid check or other financial support
- Using your social security number to obtain loans without your permission
- Using your child's social security number to claim an income tax refund without your permission
- Maxing out your credit cards without your permission
- Refusing to provide you with money, food, rent, medicine, or clothing
- Using funds from your children's tuition or a joint savings account without your knowledge
- Spending money on themselves while preventing you from doing the same
- Giving you presents or paying for things with the expectation of something in return
- Using financial circumstances to control you

metamorworks /shutterstock.com

SURVIVOR STORY: TONYA RAPLEY

Tonya Rapley was in her last two years of college when she started dating her boyfriend. The first assault came six months after she started dating him. Yet, like many survivors of domestic violence, Rapley wrote off her boyfriend's attack as a fluke incident. Things just got heated. It wouldn't happen again. She wasn't being abused. After all, it was his aggressiveness that initially attracted Rapley. Confidence can be sexy. Violence, on the other hand…

The next time her boyfriend got angry, she found his hands around her throat. Rapley fought back and he let go before she could lose consciousness. Abusers often escalate their violence over time, and Rapley's boyfriend fit that pattern to a T.

"I guess he got his courage then," she says.

The next time, he pulled a gun on her in order to intimidate her. It worked. Yet, she stayed. The two were living together now. Her boyfriend had moved them to Texas, even though Rapley was going to college in Miami. She continued her education online to be with him. "I had to appease him and graduate a semester late," she says. But it felt worth it to her at the time.

But it was when she found herself in the emergency room getting stitches in her eyebrow after he head-butted her—she told medical staff she had taken a bar to the forehead in the weight room—that she says she admitted to herself, "Oh, you're being abused, sweetheart."

She tried to distance herself from him, tried to put up clearer boundaries and stand up for herself. The next time he tried to break her wrist; she checked herself into a hotel. "It was the first time I took myself out of the situation and left him," she says.

But abusers are slick, manipulative, cunning. He convinced Rapley to come back. "I believed in him more than I believed in myself. I wanted to fix him. I wanted to make him happy."

Then, the isolation attempts began. "He had me disliking other women. He'd say, 'That woman tried to hit on me,' in order to make me feel like I needed to be at the top of my game." He told Rapley's friends things she'd told him in confidence, in an attempt to break up her relationships. "He would tell them I didn't want to talk to them anymore. Or that I was bad-mouthing them. My friends stopped talking to me after that."

> " IT TOOK HER ALMOST SEVEN YEARS TO PAY EVERYTHING OFF AND BEGIN TO REPAIR HER FINANCIAL HISTORY. IN THAT TIME, SHE MOVED TO NEW YORK AND BEGAN WORKING WITH A DOMESTIC VIOLENCE NONPROFIT.

It was a series of highs and lows that drove Rapley crazy. She said his demons started to consume her. She became someone she didn't recognize—stressed, unhappy, fearful. She soon found out she was pregnant, a move she thinks he orchestrated in order to get Rapley to stay with him, possibly forever. The final straw, she says, was when Rapley, who had been supporting her boyfriend financially since they moved, found out he had been stealing money from her bank account in order to buy drugs. She called her parents in North Carolina and asked them to help her escape.

"I knew if there was anywhere I would be safe, it'd be at my mom's and dad's. He wouldn't mess with them. I promised him we'd get back together after I got some stuff together for the baby." But Rapley had no intention of returning, and ultimately decided to terminate the pregnancy. She changed her phone number, all her online passwords. He tried to threaten her to come back. "There was a lot of verbal abuse," she says, before he began apologizing. "I never responded."

Though she escaped with her life, Rapley was financially ruined. Her boyfriend had driven her credit score into the ground, run up credit card debt in her name, and stolen her savings account. It took her almost seven years to pay everything off and begin to repair her financial history. In that time, she moved to New York and began working with a domestic violence nonprofit. She learned that many survivors, not surprisingly, stay with abusers because they're not able to support themselves financially on their own.

An idea was born. In 2013, she began My Fab Finance (myfabfinance.com), an online resource teaching financial empowerment, providing guidance on paying down debt, repairing credit, saving for the future, and making smart financial decisions in a relationship.

"Deprivation is not a viable strategy. I'm teaching them to save," she explains. By 2015, Rapley became one of the foremost experts in finance, turned her site into a six-figure business with a staff of four, became an author (The Money Manual), and was named "The New Face of Wealth Building" by Black Enterprise Magazine.

To those who want to be in control of their own finances, Rapley, who offers her services free of charge to fellow survivors, offers this advice: "Choose one goal to work toward instead of repairing your entire financial life. And, take advantage of the library. I got my first financial freedom book from the library!"

Tonya's story originally appeared on DomesticShelters.org. It is edited for length and reprinted with permission.

" RAPLEY, WHO OFFERS HER SERVICES FREE OF CHARGE TO FELLOW SURVIVORS, OFFERS THIS ADVICE: "CHOOSE ONE GOAL TO WORK TOWARD INSTEAD OF REPAIRING YOUR ENTIRE FINANCIAL LIFE. AND, TAKE ADVANTAGE OF THE LIBRARY. I GOT MY FIRST FINANCIAL FREEDOM BOOK FROM THE LIBRARY!"

IMPORTANT INFORMATION

Financial abuse is usually coupled with emotional or physical abuse. If you're not in control of your finances or if your partner has taken money from your bank account, it can be especially scary to leave an abusive relationship. Identify local resources to help you regain control over your finances—some organizations may even provide short-term loans to cover important expenses while leaving an abusive relationship.

You can also consider talking to a trusted friend, family member, or legal professional about getting a protection order. No matter what you decide to do, consider making a safety plan that includes setting aside funds in a separate, private location.

HOLD ON
TO YOUR
TRUTH

DIGITAL

WHAT IS DIGITAL ABUSE?

Digital abuse is the use of technologies like texting and social media to bully, harass, stalk, or intimidate a partner. This behavior is often a form of verbal or emotional abuse conducted online.

All communication in a healthy relationship is respectful, whether in person, online, or over the phone. It's never okay for your partner to use words or actions to harm you, lower your self-esteem, or manipulate you.

EXAMPLES OF DIGITAL ABUSE INCLUDE

- Telling you who you can or can't follow or be friends with on social media
- Sending you negative, insulting, or threatening messages or emails
- Using social media to track your activities
- Insulting and humiliating you in their posts online, including posting unflattering photos and videos
- Sending, requesting, or pressuring you to send unwanted explicit photos or videos, sexts, or otherwise compromising messages
- Stealing or pressuring you to share your account passwords
- Constantly texting you or making you feel like you can't be separated from your phone
- Looking through your phone or checking up on your pictures, texts, and phone records
- Using any kind of technology (such as spyware or GPS in a car or phone) to monitor your activities

VGstockstudio /shutterstock.com

SURVIVOR STORY: AMY BALLON

Abusive partners are known for love-bombing—they'll sweep a survivor right off their feet in a way that might seem overly romantic at first but is actually intended to start a cycle of gaslighting and dependence on the abuser.

It's how Amy Beth Ballon's relationship started with her husband. By their second date, he was calling her a princess. He even brought her a tiara. He sent flowers to her mother on Ballon's birthday, thanking her for Ballon's existence. "It was over the top," she says. She knows this now, but in the moment, it was flattering. Ballon says she felt safer with him than with anyone else she'd ever known. She had no idea it was all a setup.

Ballon and her now ex-husband, Mike,* met during a night out in Florida in 2011 when the two were dining at the same restaurant. He was a former police officer working in human resources. Ballon, a successful real estate developer, was forty-six at the time and divorced. Her two children were nearly grown— her youngest daughter was just graduating from high school—and Ballon was open to the idea of meeting and potentially marrying someone new. So, when this charming man asked her out, she accepted.

"He was just the nice guy, but he came on strong," she remembers, now calling the way he charmed his way into everyone's life "typical sociopathic behavior." Soon, she found the first crack in his seemingly perfect facade.

"He lied to me about being single. I had a suspicion … his stories didn't make sense. I finally found out he was married." He told Ballon he was getting a divorce, but she said she wouldn't believe it unless she heard it from his wife herself. Which she did. "Later I found out he bullied her into messaging me online." His ex-wife also later revealed to Ballon that Mike had once given her a gun and encouraged her to kill herself. But Ballon didn't know that when she accepted Mike's marriage proposal in February of 2012.

Mike's likable personality changed immediately after the couple married. His once romantic pet names for Ballon turned into degrading insults, once calling her a "f***ing c*nt" after a few drinks. His verbal abuse reached beyond Ballon—his tirades were aimed at women in general, including his ex-wife and the three children he shared custody of. That, and Mike's increasing distrust of Ballon, was beginning to scare her.

"He installed spyware on everything I owned," she says, a fact she would find out much later. She'd also come to discover he had installed spyware on her nineteen-year-old daughter's computer. While away at college, the camera light on her computer, her daughter told Ballon, would come on randomly.

Yet it was Ballon who caught her husband looking at an online dating site targeted at married men. Soon enough, Ballon decided it was over and asked him to move out of their condo. "The threats were crazy at that point," she says. Mike even told one of Ballon's daughters that her mom was suicidal, even though Ballon very much wasn't. She wondered, was it an ominous threat of what could happen to her?

As abusers tend to do, Mike charmed his way back into Ballon's good graces. He couldn't find a place to live, so Ballon let him stay in their condo a bit longer. On October 27, 2014, Mike offered to take Ballon out to dinner where he both accused Ballon of cheating on him and also begged her to give him another chance. It culminated in an argument, the final straw.

"I told him it's over, I'm done. I couldn't deal with it anymore."

The two went home. Ballon had just laid down in her bed when she saw Mike, six-feet tall and over two hundred pounds, rush into her bedroom in a violent rage. He jumped on top of Ballon, ramming his knee into the side of her body. She was able to reach her phone but Mike knocked her down to the floor and wrestled it away from her. Managing to get free, Ballon ran to the kitchen where she knew there was another phone, but Mike was right behind her and got to her first. He put her in what she calls "a cop hold"—his hand over her head and his thumb pushed against her windpipe. She passed out.

"I was slowly coming to when I saw him throw my phone off the balcony," Ballon says. She was able to get up and escape out the front door of their condo, making it to the front desk of the building where she called 911. Mike was predictably right behind her, except now he was yelling for someone to call an ambulance. "On the 911 call, you can hear me say, 'Oh my god, he stabbed himself.'"

With his arm bleeding, Mike met the first responder as soon as the ambulance arrived, giving them two pieces of information: (1) he was a former cop, and (2) Ballon had stabbed him. Before she could get a word out, police were next to Ballon, informing her that she was under arrest. She says they never even asked for her version of events.

"There was no blood on me. They didn't take my pajamas as evidence. They didn't read me my rights." She sat in a jail cell for fourteen hours before finding out she was being charged with assault with a deadly weapon. "It's right under manslaughter. I was facing fifteen years."

When Ballon got to the courtroom for arraignment, she says the judge looked at her charges, then looked at her. "You could see how perplexed he was," she says. Ballon had no criminal record and she says her neck still showed red marks from where her husband had strangled her. Her bail was set at $10,000, and Ballon was able to get out of jail at least temporarily. She immediately set out to fight the charges, which turned out to be more difficult than she could have ever imagined.

It turned out, the night she spent in jail Mike broke into her LinkedIn profile and disseminated her mugshot to almost every one of her 3,000-plus professional contacts. She set into motion a plan to defend herself, but adds she realizes how privileged she was to be able to do that. . . .

Ballon hired an independent forensics team. . . . She voluntarily took a polygraph test, which she passed. She took her computer to a company that discovered spyware had been installed on everything she used. . . .

Over a year after the incident, she finally had her day in court, only her husband was nowhere to be found. She says the prosecuting attorney told the judge Mike had said he wasn't coming. "Because he knew he was lying and didn't want to get caught," suspects Ballon. . . . The prosecutor decided to drop the [charges]. It was a major win for Ballon. . . .

She decided to do two things: tell her story publicly (she spent the next year writing a tell-all memoir, Fabulous to Framed) and file a malicious prosecution lawsuit against her now ex-husband. . . . She [later] decided to drop the civil suit.

Ballon has tried to move on since all of this, using her traumatic experiences to help others. She's become an outspoken advocate and public speaker, a board trustee of the Domestic Violence Advocacy Center in Florida, and has started her own nonprofit, Raising Awareness for the Innocent, to help survivors across the country who are falsely accused of a crime. She hasn't heard from Mike since the case was cleared and isn't holding her breath for an apology.

"Women who go through what I've gone through, there's such shame with being arrested and being accused of a heinous crime. But one thing I learned is that it's not your shame to bare. You hold on to your truth."

*Last name withheld for safety

Amy's story originally appeared on DomesticShelters.org. It is edited for length and reprinted with permission.

IMPORTANT INFORMATION

You never deserve to be mistreated, online or in person. If you've experienced digital dating abuse, contact a parent, teacher, or the police. Remember these truths:

- Your partner should respect your relationship boundaries. Always.
- You never have to share your passwords with anyone.
- You never have to send any explicit pictures, videos, or messages that you're uncomfortable sending ("sexting").
- Sexting can have legal consequences: nude photos or videos of someone under the age of eighteen could be considered child pornography, which is illegal to own or distribute.
- It's OK to turn off your phone or not respond to messages right away. You have the right to your own privacy and to spend time with other people without your partner getting angry. Just be sure that the people who might need to reach you in an emergency still have a way to do so.
- Save or document threatening messages, photos, videos, or voicemails as evidence of abuse.
- Don't answer calls from unknown or blocked numbers; your abuser may try calling you from another line if they suspect that you're avoiding them. Find out if your phone company allows you to block numbers (and how many, if so).
- Once you share a post or message, it's no longer under your control. Abusive partners may save or forward anything you share, so be careful sending content you wouldn't want others to see.
- Know and understand your privacy settings. Social media platforms allow users to control how their information is shared and who has access to it. These settings are often customizable and may be found in the privacy section of the website. Keep in mind that some apps require you to change your privacy settings in order to use them.
- Be mindful when checking in at places online, either by sharing your location in a post or by posting a photo with distinguishable backgrounds.
- Ask your friends to always seek permission from you before posting content online that could compromise your privacy. Do the same for them.
- Avoid contact with your abuser in any capacity, through any technology, online or in person. Consider changing your phone number if the abuse and harassment don't stop.

BE FORGIVING OF YOURSELF AS YOU HEAL

STALKING

WHAT IS STALKING?

Stalking occurs when someone watches, follows, or harasses you repeatedly, making you feel afraid or unsafe.

EXAMPLES OF STALKING INCLUDE

While the legal definition of stalking varies from state to state, these are some examples of stalking behavior:

- Showing up at your home or workplace unannounced or uninvited
- Sending you unwanted texts, messages, letters, emails, or voicemails
- Leaving you unwanted items, gifts, or flowers
- Calling you and hanging up repeatedly or making unwanted phone calls to you, your employer, a professor, or a loved one
- Using social media or technology to track your activities
- Spreading rumors about you online or in person
- Manipulating other people to investigate your life, including using someone else's social media account to look at your profile or befriending your friends in order to get information about you
- Waiting around at places you spend time
- Damaging your home, car, or property
- Hiring a private investigator to follow you as a way of knowing your location or movements

KieferPix /shutterstock.com

SURVIVOR STORY:
JESSICA HOUSTON

Jessica Houston was a bright teenager, despite her tumultuous childhood. She managed to graduate from high school a year early even after being sexually abused as a child and growing up in poverty.

During her first year of college at seventeen, Houston met a football player on campus, who would quickly become her boyfriend—and then her abuser. Houston says her low self-esteem at the time caused her to overlook early warning signs. "In the beginning of the relationship, I saw some red flags," Houston says. "He was very possessive. He didn't initially start hitting me, but he did question what I was wearing or want me to check in with him often. Me being naive, I just thought he really, really liked me."

Jessica's perspective was not dissimilar from many college-age people being abused. In fact, 70 percent do not realize when they are in a relationship with an abusive partner, according to Knowledge Networks and its "College Dating Violence and Abuse" survey.

Shortly thereafter, Jessica's boyfriend started stalking her. "I would catch him following me, or he'd pop up somewhere when I was out to eat with my friends. He'd peek into my classrooms to make sure I was there. He even climbed trees to look in my dorm room window," she says.

About three months into the relationship is when Houston's abusive boyfriend first put hands on her. He grabbed her and pushed her for wearing something he thought was too revealing. "I changed my clothes and that was the end of it," Houston says. And another three months went by. "It kind of escalated little by little," she says. "It was probably six months before he really hit me. I think he was testing the waters."

Her boyfriend starting using violence more frequently, and Houston grew more and more frightened. "It was scary, because I didn't know when he was going to strike," she says. "A lot of times, I felt like it was my fault. So I would tell myself things like 'I did stay out too long' or 'I was talking to a guy.' I was always looking over my shoulder. He ended up coming to a concert that my friends and I attended. He purchased a ticket simply to see what I was doing."

Houston endured his abuse all throughout her college career. It subsided some when she moved back home after graduation to pursue her master's degree in social work. "He would still stalk me, but the violence wasn't as bad because I was living back home," she says.

That bit of distance allowed Houston to begin planning her escape. She tried several times to break things off. "When I did try to break it off with him, he would pop back up and do something to interfere with me moving on. He'd do something like put sugar in my gas tank so I couldn't go out," she says.

Finally, after earning her master's degree, Houston found a way out. "It took me finishing my master's degree and getting a job in another state," she says. "I still loved him and I knew if I stayed anywhere near him, I'd go back. He begged and pleaded for a while, but he eventually got it. I just wanted to be free."

Today, Houston's life is vastly different, though she says it took about six years after the abuse ended to get her self-esteem back. She now holds a PhD, has a published book under her belt (Women's Secrets), and owns an organization called Expecting Victory (expectingvictory.com), whose purpose is to help women fulfill their personal goals.

"I help women push through their fears and build confidence so they can experience authentic happiness," she says. "There are often a lot of issues and pain that keep women from happiness in life. I help them address their barriers to happiness."

Jessica's story originally appeared on DomesticShelters.org. It is edited for length and reprinted with permission.

> " I STILL LOVED HIM AND I KNEW IF I STAYED ANYWHERE NEAR HIM, I'D GO BACK. HE BEGGED AND PLEADED FOR A WHILE, BUT HE EVENTUALLY GOT IT. I JUST WANTED TO BE FREE.

IMPORTANT INFORMATION

- If you're being stalked, you're likely going through a lot of stress, vulnerability, anxiety, and other emotions you may not be able to express right now, which in turn may be affecting your sleep or concentration at work or school. Every year, 3.4 million people in the US experience stalking—youths between the ages of 18 and 24 experience the highest rates.

- Most people assume that stalkers are strangers, but in reality, three out of four victims of stalking are harassed by someone they know. If you think you may be in danger, contact an emergency service provider to help you reach a safer place, and consider obtaining a protection order to prevent your stalker from coming near you. Understand the risks of contacting law enforcement for your own safety and others, including that the person harassing you may ultimately be arrested and convicted within the criminal legal system.

- Regardless of whether you intend to pursue legal action against your stalker, it's important to save evidence of the abuse for proof in the future if you ever need it. Take time to write down the dates, times, and places of each incident that occurred, including names and contact information for people who may have witnessed what happened. Here are some examples of such evidence:
  - Text messages
  - Voicemails
  - Pictures or videos
  - Letter, photographs, or cards
  - Unwanted items or gifts
  - Social media harassment (including inappropriate friend or follow requests)

- Stalking is a traumatic experience. You may lose sleep, feel depressed, have nightmares, or feel like you don't have control over your life because of your experience. These reactions are normal and you should be forgiving of yourself as you heal. It can help to tell a trusted friend or loved one about your experience and work to develop a safety plan.

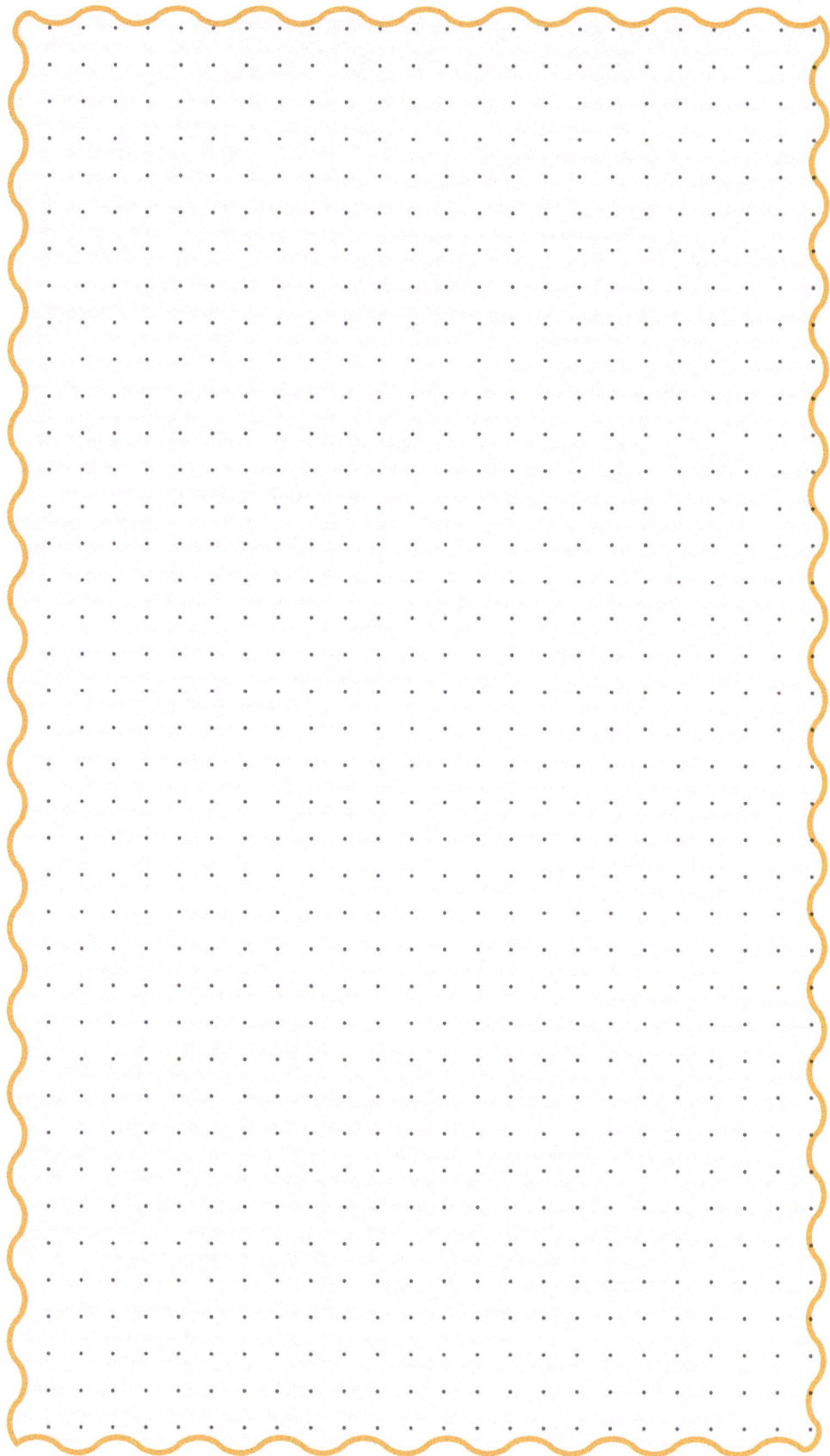

THREAD TALK WORD SEARCH

Find the following words in the puzzle.
Words are hidden horizontally and vertically.

ALEXIS, HOPE, WONDER, CONFIDENCE, LUISA, COURAGE, LOVE, RESILIENCE,
HANNAH KAY, SERENITY, HAPPINESS, STRENGTH, THREAD TALK

A	L	F	P	J	J	V	D	L	H	E	E	S
X	L	L	U	I	S	A	B	Z	V	I	K	W
C	I	E	G	U	Q	Q	B	O	X	L	S	D
O	F	N	X	O	J	U	L	E	A	U	J	H
U	H	L	E	I	W	R	L	T	O	X	H	A
R	J	V	K	R	S	A	D	X	J	T	C	N
A	S	H	O	P	E	A	L	M	G	T	O	N
G	S	A	Q	G	E	S	W	N	Y	R	N	A
E	E	D	C	R	E	P	E	T	A	W	F	H
S	N	O	H	B	N	R	L	X	N	P	I	K
H	I	T	Y	B	T	Q	L	N	J	B	D	A
N	P	R	E	S	I	L	I	E	N	C	E	Y
X	P	S	Z	G	A	E	V	T	N	I	N	S
M	A	U	N	C	C	T	E	H	E	Z	C	K
V	H	V	R	E	D	N	O	W	C	D	E	A
C	K	Q	P	L	B	P	B	E	Z	C	I	X
S	E	R	E	N	I	T	Y	N	B	D	I	D

CHAPTER FOUR

WAYS TO SUPPORT SOMEONE IN AN ABUSIVE RELATIONSHIP

Many of us have been or will be affected by an abusive relationship, whether we're the ones in the relationship or someone we know is being impacted. Abusive relationships can come in many forms. If you see someone acting strange while around their partner, keep an eye out for their safety. Strange behaviors can include not being able to hang out as much as they used to, being cautious about what they do or search online, flinching at sudden movements, and the list goes on. Sometimes, the person being abused feels as if they can't ask for help.

Here are ways you can aid them without sparking the attention of their abuser:

- Ask them to meet for lunch and discuss things.
- Try and help them find a healthy way to leave their partner.
- Provide them with a place to stay.
- Make sure that they know that you are always available for them.

These are just a few ways to help someone in an abusive relationship. Remember, you can make a big difference in someone's life with a small gesture of showing that you care.

DON'T
- Judge
- Blame
- Immediately tell them to break up
- Try to force them to break up
- Jump to solutions
- Give ultimatums

DO
- Listen first
- Acknowledge feelings
- Be supportive
- Try to understand what they are going through

EDUCATE YOURSELF

Gather all information you can about domestic violence—you are already off to a great start with this guide! Sometimes your feelings about violence may make it difficult for you to confront the situation.

LEND A SYMPATHETIC EAR

Let your friends know that you care and are willing to listen. Do not force the conversation. However, when your friends are ready to confide in you, allow them to come and talk to you. Keep your heart open and be ready to listen to what your friends say to you.

BE NONJUDGMENTAL

Never blame, criticize, or guilt your friends for what's happening or underestimate your friend's fear of potential danger. Remember that your friend must make their own decisions about their life. Focus on supporting your friend's right to make their own choices and decisions.

SAFETY PLANNING

Encourage your friend to protect themself by developing a personalized plan. Help your friend think through the steps to take if their abuser becomes violent again. Make a list of people your friend can call in an emergency. Suggest that your friend put together and hide a suitcase of clothing, personal items, money, social security cards, and other important documents. Offer to keep their suitcase at your house if you are able.

CHAPTER FIVE

SAFETY PLANNING

SAFETY AT SCHOOL

1. A trusted adult, teacher, coach, or counselor I can talk to about my relationship is

   _____

2. The safest form of transportation to and from class is

   _____

3. If I need to have my schedule changed or need help with avoiding my partner at school I can talk to

   _____

4. If I need someone to walk me to and from class or the parking lot I can ask

   _____

5. Safe places I can go to at school are

   _____

SAFETY AT HOME

6. Someone in my family that I can talk to about my relationship is

   _____

7. If my roommates aren't home, I will ask _____ and _____ to stay with me at home until they come back.

8. In an emergency situation I can exit my house through

   _____

9. If I have to leave in an emergency, I will go to a safe location such as

   _____

10. I will tell my roommates or parents about this location ahead of time. ☐

11. I will create a code word to alert my friends, family, and neighbors to call for help. The code word will be _____

12. I will only share this codeword with people I trust. ☐

GENERAL SAFETY TIPS

- Keep your cellphone charged and with you at all times. Add any important numbers to your contacts. If you don't feel safe adding an agency's name, create a safe name to store the contact under.
- Tell a family member or friend where you are going and what you are doing.
- Use the buddy system and try your best to never go anywhere alone.
- Try not to go places alone in the dark.
- Change up your schedule and routine.
- Try to avoid places that you and your ex-partner would go together.
- Call 911 if you feel unsafe.
- Keep the doors and windows locked to your home. Always make sure you know who is at the door before you answer it.
- Be aware of resources in your community.
- Look into seeking a protection order if you have safety concerns.
- Remember that the abuse is not your fault; you deserve to be in a safe, happy, and healthy relationship.

SAFETY DURING AND AFTER A BREAKUP

- If you don't feel safe ending the relationship in person, end it over the phone. It may seem cruel to break up over the phone, but your safety is the most important thing.
- If you are going to break up in person, do so in a public place. You may want to bring a friend along for safety.
- You do not need to explain more than once why you are ending the relationship. You do not owe your ex-partner an explanation.
- Let a family member or friend know you are ending the relationship and when you plan on doing it.
- Make teachers or counselors aware of your safety concerns. They may even be able to help you change your schedule.
- Block your ex-partner's social media accounts and phone number.
- Change any passwords or account information your ex-partner may have access to.
- Use the buddy system or ask a security guard to walk you to and from your car.
- Ask friends and family to not tag you in pictures on social media or ask them to not post the location of where you are hanging out.
- Ask mutual friends to not share private details about your life with your ex-partner.

CHAPTER SIX

DOMESTIC VIOLENCE SHELTERS AND PROGRAMS NEAR YOU

DomesticShelters.org

Visit DomesticShelters.org for a domestic violence shelter, hotline, or program closest to you. DomesticShelters.org makes it easier to locate the right shelter and to find information about domestic violence. Instead of searching the internet, it is all right on the website. They've painstakingly verified information on shelters from Los Angeles to New York, and every domestic violence program in between. If you or a friend is suffering from physical abuse, emotional abuse, psychological abuse, or verbal abuse, this free service can help. Select domestic violence programs based on location, service, and language needs. Find 24-hour hotlines in your area; service listings; helpful articles on domestic violence statistics; signs and cycles of abuse; housing services; emergency services; legal and financial services; support groups for women, children, and families; and more.

love is respect
24/7/365 phone, chat & text support
Available in English & Spanish
Anonymous & Confidential

Call: 1-866-331-9474
Text: LOVEIS to 22522
Chat: loveisrespect.org

A few select domestic violence shelters and programs based on region

West
Abused Women's Aid In Crisis, Inc. (AWAIC), Anchorage, AK
907-272-0100
www.awaic.org

Stand Up Placer, Auburn, CA
800-575-5352
standupplacer.org

A Woman's Place, Greeley, CO
970-356-4226
www.awpdv.org

Southwest
Sojourner Center, Phoenix, AZ
602-244-0089
www.sojournercenter.org

The Family Place, Dallas, TX
214-941-1991
www.familyplace.org

Houston Area Women Center, Houston, TX
713-528-2121
www.hawc.org

Enlace Comunitario, Albuquerque, NM
505-246-8972
www.enlacenm.org

Midwest
WINGS Program, Inc., Palatine, IL
847-221-5680
www.wingsprogram.com

SafeCenter, St. Johns, MI
877-952-7283
Thesafecenter.org

Newhouse Inc., Kansas City, MO
816-471-5800
www.newhousekc.org

Sojourner Family Peace Center, Milwaukee, WI
414-933-2722
www.familypeacecenter.org

Southeast
Northwest Arkansas Women's Shelter, Rogers, AR
479-246-9999
www.nwaws.org

Peaceful Paths Domestic Violence Network, Gainesville, FL
352-377-8255
www.peacefulpaths.com

Tapestri, Tucker, GA
404-299-2185
www.tapestri.org/domestic-violence

GreenHouse17, Lexington, KY
800-544-2022
www.greenhouse17.org

Laurens County Safe Home, Clinton, SC
864-682-7270
www.thesafehome.org

Samaritan House, Inc., Virginia Beach, VA
757-251-0144
www.samaritanhouseva.org

Northeast
District Alliance for Safe Housing (DASH), Washington, DC
202-462-3274
www.dashdc.org

Inge Benevolent Ministries Muslimat Al Nisaa Shelter, Baltimore, MD
410-466-8686
www.mnisaashelter.org

Barrier Free Living, New York, NY
212-400-6470
www.bflnyc.org

Women's Center & Shelter of Greater Pittsburgh, Pittsburgh, PA
412-687-8005
www.wcspittsburgh.org

CHAPTER SEVEN

THE IMPORTANCE OF JOURNALING

Developing a journaling habit can be very beneficial for a myriad of different reasons. Journaling helps keep your mental and spiritual health aligned while also allowing you to reflect on your day-to-day life. It can help aid the development of your identity and nurture new insights. Journaling is a useful tool for self-growth and helps people all over the world.

USE THE FOLLOWING PAGES AS YOU
WISH TO JOURNAL WHAT IS ON YOUR
HEART, MIND & SOUL

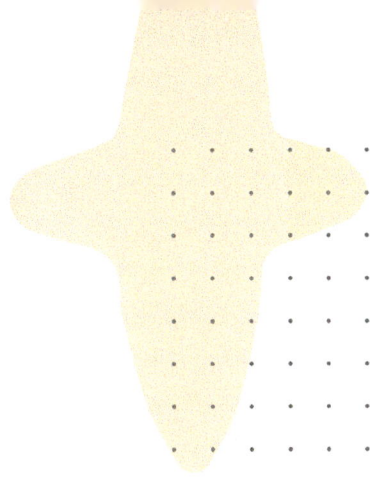

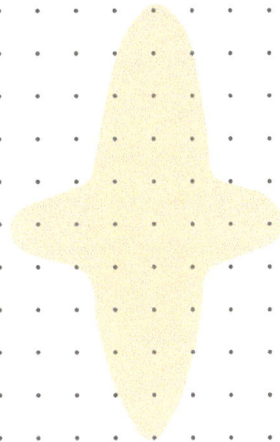

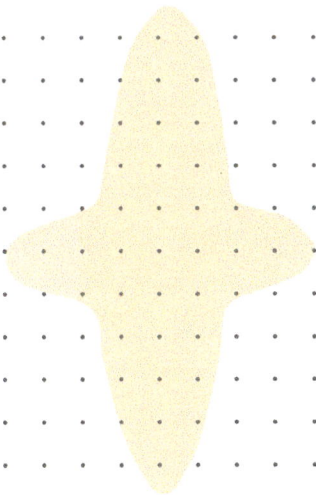

_____
_____
_____
_____
_____
_____
_____
_____
_____
_____
_____
_____
_____
_____
_____
_____
_____
_____

YOU ARE STRONG

YOU ARE LOVED

YOU ARE NOT ALONE

KEEP IN TOUCH WITH THREAD TALK

WWW.THREADTALK.COM

@THREADTALKSTRONG

HELLO@THREADTALK.COM

www.ingramcontent.com/pod-product-compliance
Lightning Source LLC
Chambersburg PA
CBHW042337030426
42335CB00028B/3370